Footnotes

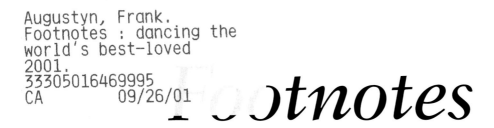

Footnotes

DANCING THE WORLD'S BEST-LOVED BALLETS

Frank Augustyn
and Shelley Tanaka

The Millbrook Press Brookfield, Connecticut

All quotes were taken from tapes made for the *Footnotes* television series, with the exception of the following: pp. 57, 58. O.Wilkins as quoted by Paula Citron in "Upbeat: Ormsby Wilkins and the Fine Art of Conducting," *Performance*. Dec. 1995-Feb. 1996. pp. 23, 26; p. 63, M. Lehman as quoted by John Marcus in the *Toronto Star*, July 13, 1997; p. 69, Tchaikovsky as quoted by Martin Feinstein in the Royal Ballet souvenir program, 1963; p. 86, K. Kain as quoted by John Fraser in *Kain & Augustyn* (Macmillan, 1977), p. 98; p. 87, Darcey Bussell, *The Young Dancer* (Dorling Kindersley, 1995), p. 53.

Photo Credits:
Pages: 3, 8, 17, 32, 39, 40, 44, 47, 59, 82, 84, 86 (top right), 91 (upper), 93. © The National Ballet of Canada; Pages: 11, 13, 81, 83, 86 © Lydia Pawelak/The National Ballet of Canada; Page 16 © David Street/The National Ballet of Canada; Pages: 22, 26, 36, 52 (top), 57, 62, 68, 70, 73, 74 © Cylla von Tiedemann/The National Ballet of Canada; Pages: 38, 42 © Andrew Oxenham/The National Ballet of Canada; Page10 © Barry Lewis/CORBIS; Page 12 © Steve Raymer/CORBIS; Page 21 (top) © Gianni Dagli/CORBIS; Page 27 © John Garrett/CORBIS; Page 58 © Barry Lewis/CORBIS; Pages: 17 (top), 21 (bottom), 23 (left), 31, 45, 61, 69, 80, 89, 91 © Culver Pictures Inc; Pages: 14, 48, 49, 51, 71 © Todd Korol Photography; Page 18 © Laurence Acland; Pages: 19, 65, 76, 86, 90, 92 © Linda Vartoogian; Pages: 23 (right), 24, 29, 34, 43, 44, 53, 54, 60, 67, 75, 77, 78, 85, 86 (top, left) © Jack Vartoogian; Page 28 (top) © David Cooper/Royal Winnipeg Ballet; Pages: 33, 35, 72 © Martha Swope/TimePix; Page 86 © Gjon Mili/TimePix; Pages: 52 (bottom), 56 © Trudie Lee/Alberta Ballet.

Published in 2001 by The Millbrook Press, Inc.
2 Old New Milford Road, Brookfield, Connecticut 06804
www.millbrookpress.com

First published in Canada in 2001 by
Key Porter Books Limited
70 The Esplanade
Toronto, Ontario
Canada M5E 1R2
www.keyporter.com

Text copyright © 2001 by Sound Venture Productions Ottawa Limited and Frank Augustyn Productions Inc. and Shelley Tanaka.

Inspired by the television series *Footnotes: The Classics of Ballet*, co-produced by Sound Ventures Productions Ottawa Ltd. And Frank Augustyn Productions Inc.

The Library of Congress Control Number: 00-050075
ISBN 0-7613-2323-6

Design: Peter Maher
Electronic formatting: John Lightfoot

5 4 3 2 1

Printed and bound in Singapore

For young dancers everywhere

ACKNOWLEDGMENTS

It is particularly appropriate to note that in this book there is no such thing as a solitary endeavor.

Though there is not enough room here to thank everyone who played a role in creating the *Footnotes* television series upon which this book is based, as well as the book itself, I am very grateful for their participation.

First and foremost I would like to thank Shelley Tanaka for her exquisite adaptation from screen to page. Her innate understanding of a world she was not completely familiar with is testament to her intelligence and sensitivity.

Andrea Bock has been a thoughtful and patient editor who encouraged me to revisit the dancer as a human being.

Thanks to Dianne Broad, the copy editor, who added to the manuscript her eye for detail.

I would also like to thank all the talented individuals — the dancers, critics and directors — who contributed to the making of the *Footnotes* television series. In particular I would like to thank executive producer Neil Bregman without whose superior business and organizational acumen the series never would have been produced.

To Michael Levine, Jan Whitford, Moses Znaimer and Paul Gratton who were one hundred percent behind this project from the very beginning, thank-you.

Derek Diorio and Katherine Jeans, the directors of the episodes, were central in developing a cohesive and entertaining program. To them I express my gratitude.

Writers Dan Lalande and Michael Laewen, both of whom I could not do without, my heartfelt thank-you.

Thanks to my production crew and staff, too numerous to mention, for their guidance, expertise and hard work. I admire and respect you all.

And finally, this book would never have been possible without the support of my loving family — my wife Erene and our two children, Kyra and Nicholas.

FRANK AUGUSTYN

Contents

Introduction

When I was eleven years old, my parents took me to the Palace Theatre in Hamilton, Ontario, to see a ballet called *La Sylphide*. I had never been inside a real theater before, and everything about it struck me as rich and exotic. I leaned my head back on the plush velvet seat and gazed up at the dim lights flickering off the crystal chandelier far above me. I listened to the shreds of melody and mysterious scrapes and scuffling coming from the musicians hidden in the orchestra pit. I heard the rustling of programs and murmurs as the audience slowly filtered in. The women were freshly permed and smiling; the men in suits, not smiling quite as much, were close behind them. The buzz grew louder and more animated, and soon every seat in the house was filled.

The majestic Opera House in Budapest, Hungary

Finally the lights abruptly dimmed and we were plunged into blackness. A hush fell over the room, someone coughed, and there was silence.

The performance began.

I'd never seen anything like it. I kept expecting the dancers to speak or sing, but they did neither. Instead, they spoke through movement, and I found myself entranced by this new language. It was a language that I could completely understand.

When the performance was over, my mind was made up. I was going to be a dancer.

After that I trained long and hard for many years and I did, in fact, become a ballet dancer. During my career I have danced most of the major classical ballets on stages around the world, and I've been lucky enough to partner with some of the foremost ballerinas of our time, including Karen Kain, Cynthia Gregory, Gelsey Kirkland and Marianna Tcherkassky. I've also had the extraordinary good fortune to work with two of the greatest ballet masters of this century, Erik Bruhn and Rudolf Nureyev. In fact it was Nureyev who gave me the break of my life by casting me as the prince in *The Sleeping Beauty* when I was only nineteen. I have also met and become friends with several of the world's finest dancers, many of whom have contributed to the *Footnotes* TV series and to this book.

This ballet class is being held outdoors and the bright sun has some of the dancers practicing in sunglasses.

Over the years I've experienced every side of this amazing art form — as a student, a performer, an artistic director and as a teacher and I've witnessed many magical moments: a ballerina waiting in the wings for her umpteenth performance as Juliet, her eyes filling with tears yet again as she hears the familiar strains of Prokofiev's beautiful music; the amazing Jennifer Gelfand of the Boston Ballet performing nine pirouettes in a row at a gala in Japan (on pointe — *after* doing thirty-two fouettés); an audience leaping to its feet in applause after a performance of *Giselle* so perfect the dancers seemed to be carried through by an unknown force.

Ballerinas watch the
performance as they wait
for their cue.

And I've witnessed some not-so-magical moments, too. Like the time the Mouse King's banner fell on my head during a performance of *The Nutcracker*, and I was rushed to the hospital in my Prince costume. Or the night a man ran stark naked across the stage at New York's Metropolitan Opera House in the middle of Nureyev's performance (and to the dancer's delight) in *The Sleeping Beauty*. I've seen ballerinas jetéing into the orchestra pit, a conductor waving his arms with such gusto that he stuck his baton through his thumb, even a flock of birds landing on the stage of an outdoor theater during the White Swan's pas de deux in *Swan Lake*.

The bridesmaids in
Romeo and Juliet

Despite its ethereal illusions, ballet also has its all-too-real side. After all, dancers are real people who mow their lawns and have bad-hair days just like anyone else. But I'm convinced that dancers are exceptional, too. They dedicate their bodies and minds to the most physically and emotionally demanding of all the performing arts, and they do it to create something extraordinary — the magic and beauty of the great classic ballets.

I hope that one day you will feel some of this magic, too. Maybe you'll see a ballet and find that you're paying more attention to the dancers than you are to the story. Maybe you'll struggle to master a step in ballet class and suddenly realize that the young Margot Fonteyn started in just the same way. Or maybe you'll find yourself with a lump in your throat as you listen to the closing chords of *Swan Lake*'s music.

Or maybe, as you read about the stories, history and performances that lie behind the great classic ballets, you too will share some of that very same passion that inspires all dancers.

FRANK AUGUSTYN

La Sylphide

Ballet Goes Up on Its Toes

Ah, the ballet. Delicate women on tiptoe in fluffy white skirts. Muscled and lean young men in tights doing impossible leaps. A gold and red theater with velvet seats. Mournful violin music pouring from an orchestra pit.

And all for a crowd of stuffy rich people dripping with jewels and furs.

How did ballet get this highbrow reputation as the art of the wealthy and privileged? Mozart's operas and Shakespeare's plays were first performed in noisy open-air theaters and enjoyed by audiences from all classes and backgrounds, and ballet is, if anything, even more accessible than theater. The stories are simple tales of love, jealousy and magic. Many are based on popular fairy tales. There are no Italian librettos to follow, no complicated histories to understand.

Yet it is true that in seventeenth-century France, ballets were designed principally for the entertainment of the court. They were part of a *long* evening (usually five hours or more) of dance, music and poetry performed for the king's entertainment.

Dancers may use up to four different pairs of pointe shoes during a single performance — soft, broken-in shoes for scenes with a lot of jumps so they don't make much noise on landing; harder, newer shoes for scenes with turns and balances.

Those seventeenth-century ballets didn't look like much. The men (in those days it was considered indecent for women to dance in public) wore tall headdresses, wigs, elaborate suits and pointy, high-heeled shoes, but they did little more than walk elegantly about the floor.

It wasn't until France's King Louis XIV (who considered himself to be quite a talented dancer and performed in his first ballet at the age of thirteen) singled out dance for special attention that it began to resemble the ballet we know today. Under his instruction the Académie Royale de Danse (a professional organization for dancing masters) was established and the five positions of the feet were invented, as well as the set positions for the body, arms, head — even the eyes. Before long France became the center of the dance world, and French became the universal language of ballet.

In the beginning all the dancers were men, and men wearing masks would dance the women's roles. It wasn't until 1681 that the first female dancers performed professionally in a theater production, appearing in a ballet called *Le Triomphe de l'Amour* (*The Triumph of Love*). After that women gradually began to make more appearances on stage. At first the tight corsets and long, heavy skirts (as well as the belief that women should be modest and not exert themselves) kept their movements small and sedate. But slowly, things changed. In 1726, Marie Camargo, a famous Belgian dancer with the Paris Opera who was particularly proud of her dazzling footwork, decided to shorten her long skirt just enough to expose her shoes and the tiniest bit of ankle. Around the same time, Marie Sallé exchanged her corset, petticoats and wig for a loose robe and flowing hairstyle that combined to make her movements more natural and dramatic.

Then, in the early nineteenth century, a bizarre invention came along that changed ballet forever. The pointe shoe made ballet different from every other kind of dance in the world. It also turned the audience's eyes away from the male dancer and put the ballerina front and center.

Dancing on tiptoe first came to the world's attention at the premiere performance of *La Sylphide* in 1832. In this ballet, a sylph, a winged fairy creature, lures the hero away from his fiancée. *La Sylphide*'s choreographer, Filippo Taglioni, used every means at his disposal to create the illusion that the sylphs were supernatural creatures. Gas lights, which had just been invented, flickered off the dancers' transparent skirts like fairy dust and bathed the stage in a magical light. Wires and hidden supports lifted the dancers and made them look as if they were flying. Taglioni also chose his daughter, Maria, to play the part of the Sylphide because of her almost otherworldly light and airy dancing. Finally, he had Maria dance on her toes to give the

The Italian ballerina Maria Taglioni was chosen by her father to play the part of the Sylphide because of her light dancing.

France's King Louis XIV established the Académie Royale de Danse and the five positions of the feet, shown here, were invented.

position   Second position   Third position   Fourth position   Fifth position

Standing on pointe is an incredibly difficult feat for any ballerina. This X-ray photograph captures the painful force created when a dancer's foot is on pointe.

audience the impression that she was barely touching the stage as she moved.

Dancing on tiptoe wasn't easy for Maria. Her shoes weren't reinforced with canvas and glue the way they are today. (Instead, her father invented exercises to strengthen her feet and ankles.) And she couldn't stay up on tiptoe for very long. Still, audiences were amazed to see her glide across the stage.

Dancing on your toes is agonizing, even after years of training. The shoes take such a beating that a prima ballerina will go through several pairs in just one performance. "You never really get used to it," says Karen Kain. "The human body does not really adapt to putting those instruments of torture on your feet."

The modern pointe shoe is made of leather, satin, glue and canvas, and in large professional companies the shoes are custom-made for each and every dancer. Yet even the tiniest change can make a ballerina feel as if she is dancing in wooden clogs. "It's like that fairy tale, *The Princess and the Pea*," says Marianna Tcherkassky. "The slightest change throws off your center of gravity, your balance. And it's scary because you get shoes that you just can't dance on!"

Even when the shoes fit perfectly, they still hurt. Ballerinas have a bag full of tricks to lessen the pain (lamb's wool, plastic toe protectors, special gel-filled pouches, tape). But in the end it is only the dancer's bones and muscles that hold her on pointe. When a ballerina stands on one toe, her entire weight presses down on an area the size of a coin. No wonder it's painful!

So why don't the ballerinas of the world unite and agree to throw away their pointe shoes to spare themselves the agony? The pointe shoe is still around because ballerinas are willing to put up with the pain in order to produce something beautiful — the long line and elegant tapering of the foot that simply cannot be achieved any other way. (Dancers add to the illusion by applying pancake makeup over their satin shoes to dull the finish and mask the line between shoe and foot, a trick that skaters have adapted by matching the color of their skates to the color of their tights or pants.)

Ever since the invention of the pointe shoe, dancers have continued to dedicate body and soul to creating beauty, at agonizing cost. They cram their feet into impossible shoes and squeeze their bodies into waist-nipping tutus. They train their muscles to jump and lift and reach so they can soar across the stage without wires or supports. They smile serenely when they are in terrible pain and force their limbs into unnatural poses to form graceful positions.

Classical ballet is the most physically and emotionally grueling of all the performing arts, and it is widely known that ballet dancers are in better condition than most professional athletes. But during a sports game athletes can go to the bench when they're winded while another line takes over. They can

Mikhail Baryshnikov and Gelsey Kirkland dance in this 1975 production of
La Sylphide

La Sylphide: Synopsis

Act I

The curtain rises on a Scottish country house in the 1830s. James, a young gentleman, is to be married that afternoon to his fiancée, Effie. He sits dozing in a chair in front of a fire. Suddenly, as if in a dream, a beautiful Sylphide appears before him. She kisses James's cheek and he awakens. James is utterly entranced with her. He tries to catch her but she eludes him and disappears up the chimney.

Villagers arrive at the manor with wedding gifts. Madge, a fortune-telling witch, also appears. When she predicts that Effie will marry James's best friend, Gurn, James throws the old woman out of his house.

The sylph appears again and beckons James to follow her into the woods. When he refuses, she snatches Effie's wedding ring from his hand and runs out of the farmhouse. James runs after her. Effie pleads with the ever-faithful Gurn to find James, then collapses in a faint.

Act II

In the dark forest, six witches, led by Madge, concoct a magic brew in which they dip a white scarf. Then the forest vanishes and James enters, chasing his Sylphide. She eludes him again and again. Madge appears and gives James the magic scarf, telling him that if he wraps the scarf around his Sylphide, she will be his forever.

James eventually captures the sylph with the scarf only to discover that the witch has deceived him. The scarf's magic is evil, and the sylph dies. As she is taken away by the other sylphs, James sees a wedding procession in the distance. It is Effie, who has married Gurn. In pursuing something unearthly, James has lost his chance for happiness in the real world.

wave at the coach to pull them off the court if they've come down painfully from a jump. They can put on a burst of speed in the homestretch to make up for a slow running start. In ballet, as long as a dancer is on that stage, there is no respite. Dancers must be consistent throughout an entire performance, even though quite often the most demanding solos occur toward the end of the ballet.

Not only that, but, unlike athletes, dancers can never show their pain or exhaustion. They must create the illusion that dance is effortless by controlling their facial expressions, their emotions and their muscles.

In 1832, the audience saw a ballerina flitting across the stage as she danced on her toes for the first time in *La Sylphide*. They saw her long skirt billowing wispily around her, as fragile as mist.

The audience loved it. They wanted more. And ballet would never be the same.

For Polite Company Only?

Ballet grew out of the French court, where the rituals of behavior were as choreographed as any dance movement, and the price of violating court etiquette was banishment, or worse. But even ballet fans have been known to forget their manners from time to time. When *The Rite of Spring*, choreographed and performed by Vaslav Nijinsky, first appeared in Paris in 1913, the boos and catcalls from the disapproving audience were so loud the dancers couldn't hear the music. Fistfights broke out in the aisles.

Eventually even the dancers were drawn into the fray. Nijinsky complained that the riot was caused by Igor Stravinsky's avant-garde music. Stravinsky insisted that it was Nijinsky who'd started the trouble by making a rude gesture during the performance.

An official program of the Ballets Russes

Vaslav Nijinsky was noted for his leading roles in the Ballets Russes, founded by Serge Diaghilev. Tired of producing the traditional classics, Diaghilev hired dynamic new designers, choreographers, composers and musicians to recharge what he thought had become a stale art form.

What Do Baseball Pitchers, Cellists and Ballerinas Have in Common?

During a performance, dancers will frequently rub their shoes in a box filled with powdered or rock rosin, the same sticky substance that pitchers use on their hands to help them grip the ball and that violinists rub on their bows to keep them on the strings. Rosin increases the friction between two surfaces. It helps prevent dancers from slipping on slippery stages. (There's also such a thing as too much rosin. Some stage managers have been known to wipe the stage with a rosin-dipped mop, surprising dancers who can suddenly find that their customary six pirouettes have abruptly stopped at four! And in an open-air theater, the hot sun can turn a rosin-covered floor into a sticky mess — like dancing on a floor after someone has spilled several soft drinks!)

Jennifer Fournier of the National Ballet of Canada applies rosin to her feet before putting on her ballet slipper.

Dancers go to extreme lengths to keep their feet on the floor. They ruthlessly cut the shiny satin off the toes of new pointe shoes. They rosin the bottoms of their tights to make their feet more secure in their shoes. They'll even rub the soles of their shoes with a cheese grater to roughen the surface. No ballerina wants to slip off her pointe shoes, and a male dancer who loses his footing during a tricky lift will not be popular with either the audience or his partner!

Why Do Dancers Walk So Funny?

Two things set ballet apart from other kinds of dance: the pointe shoe and what dancers call turnout. Turnout involves rotating the legs within the hip socket so the feet and knees point out to the side. In King Louis XIV's day, a pointed and turned-out foot was considered the epitome of elegance. Turnout helped dancers create long lines that could be admired by audiences from the front. Although the precise evolution of turnout remains something of a mystery, some historians believe that it was a consequence of the royal decree that forbade anyone to turn their back on the king. As a result, dancers tended to move sideways across the floor when they were performing, their toes pointing demurely outward. However, it is also possible that turnout is a carryover from the traditional fencing stance.

Turnout is the foundation of all ballet positions. From the very beginning of a classical ballet education, young dancers work to rotate their feet and knees to the side. After years of training, this results in what is commonly known as the dancer's "duck walk," or permanently turned-out feet.

The Dancer's Body, Then and Now

The ideal dancer's body has changed a great deal over the years. One hundred years ago, most dancers were small and stocky, with well-developed calf muscles. Today's dancers are lean and long-limbed, and bulgy calves can be considered a sign of poor training.

Anna Pavlova circa 1900

Susan Jaffe in rehearsal with the American Ballet Theater

Tights and Tutus

When women first began to dance in ballets, they wore their regular clothes — stiff, floor-length hoop skirts with layers of bulky petticoats and whalebone corsets.

Darcey Bussell in the Royal Ballet production of *Prince of the Pagodas*

When Marie Camargo first shortened her skirt to expose her shoes and just the tiniest bit of ankle, she created an enormous scandal, though her sparkling footwork (she is credited with performing the first entrechat) eventually silenced her critics. Still, it was more than fifty years later before ballerinas were allowed to show any more of their legs, thanks to the invention of tights (invented by Maillot, the costume designer at the Paris Opera). Finally ballerinas could wear the long, below-the-knee tutus seen in ballets like *La Sylphide* and *Giselle* without actually showing bare skin. (The Pope himself banned skin-colored tights, because they gave the impression that the legs were naked.)

By the end of the nineteenth century, steps had become even more complicated and exact. But there wasn't much point in doing a perfectly straight-legged, high arabesque when the audience couldn't even see your knees, so the stiff, short tutu was invented to show off the ballerina's leg work and extensions.

The short tutu is a mixed blessing for dancers. During rehearsals, the ballerina wears a tutu so her partner can get used to not being able to see her legs. During lifts, the male dancer has to reach over the saucerlike skirt to support the ballerina and often ends up with a face full of gauze as a result!

Fernando Bujones got a face full of tutu when he lifted ballerina Susan Jaffe in this 1996 production of *Coppélia*

Giselle

Dancers as Storytellers

Even dancers admit that the story of *Giselle* is just plain ridiculous. A prince who nearly dances himself to death? Why would anyone pay money to see that? If the story is so silly, why is *Giselle* still one of the favorite ballets of dancers and audiences alike?

Technically, the ballet itself is not terribly difficult. The male lead, in particular, has little to do until the end of the last scene, when spirits force him to dance until he collapses. (Some dancers say that those last seven minutes more than make up for the simplicity of the rest of the ballet — "I didn't have to act like I was tired," says Kevin McKenzie of that grueling last scene. "I was exhausted. When I hit the ground I didn't think I was going to be able to get back up. I thought, use it. Maybe they'll think you're a brilliant actor!") Yet any dancer will tell you that simply doing the steps correctly is only half the job, because ballet is also about telling a story. "Every step is like a sentence, with the dancer talking to her partner or to the audience," says Cynthia Gregory.

Because there's no speaking in ballet, dancers must use mime in order to convey the feelings and explain the actions of the characters. This ballerina is using her acting skills to express sorrow and dismay.

Chan Hon Goh as Giselle in the National Ballet of Canada's production

Evelyn Hart is world renowned for her sensitive portrayal of Giselle

Giselle was the first major ballet that required dancers to also be real actors, and the melodrama and absurd plot make it even more of an acting challenge. It takes huge skill to dig below the silliness of the story and make the audience sympathize with Giselle and Albrecht. As Julie Kent says, "Who hasn't loved somebody enough that you feel as if you could just die of a broken heart, and then be able to forgive that person? It's not so unbelievable. The essence of these feelings is real."

Because there's no speaking in a ballet, dancers must use mime in order to convey feelings. Mime uses expression and gesture to tell a story. "Mime helps an audience to know exactly what's going on," explains Darcey Bussell. But good mime is not as simple as playing charades. If it's done poorly, it looks ridiculous.

In mime, some things are easier to say than others. There are

A ballerina must undergo a fast transformation to change from heart-broken maiden to Wili. Here Evelyn Hart has been transformed into the tragic spirit.

simple and beautiful gestures for love, sadness, anger and fear. But sometimes the message becomes a little more complicated. In many versions of *Giselle*, for example, Giselle's mother tells her daughter about the legend of the Wilis, maidens who have died before their weddings but come back between dusk and dawn to make men dance until they fall dead. Not an easy thing to explain using only gestures!

In fact, mime can be so difficult, many choreographers simply choose to remove it. (An early version of *Swan Lake*, for instance, contained long mime passages explaining that the lake

was made of Odette's mother's tears.) Others consider it to be unnecessary and old-fashioned, since audiences can simply refer to their programs to find out the details of the story.

Despite this, some dancers regret the loss of mime in ballet — "It's like cutting out a tune in an opera," says Antoinette Sibley.

In *Giselle*, the entire ballet hangs on the performance of the ballerina. A great ballerina must do more than dazzle the spectators with the height of her arabesques or the speed of her pirouettes. She must convince the audience that it makes perfect sense for Giselle to go mad after she discovers that the man she loves has betrayed her.

Evelyn Hart has been praised around the world for her portrayal of Giselle. In fact, she has spent her entire career studying and perfecting the complexities of this role. She says a dancer must set the stage for the mad scene from the very moment the ballet starts: "How do you let the audience know, from the second you walk through that door, the elements of your character, so that

Vanessa Harwood, as the Queen of the Wilis, faces the audience in this Universal Ballet Company production of *Giselle*

Giselle: Synopsis

Act I

In a valley surrounded by hills in medieval Germany, Count Albrecht, Duke of Silesia, disguises himself as a peasant and goes into the village during the harvest festival to join in on the festivities. He meets a beautiful peasant girl, Giselle, who immediately falls in love with him. This arouses the jealousy of the local gamekeeper, Hilarion. Albrecht and Giselle dance together joyously, even though Giselle's mother reminds her that she is not supposed to exert herself because she has a weak heart. Just as Giselle is about to be crowned queen of the harvest festival, a group of nobles arrives, including Countess Bathilde, who is revealed by Hilarion to be Albrecht's fiancée.

Giselle is devastated and goes mad with grief. Finally, she collapses and dies, leaving Albrecht distraught.

Act II

Filled with remorse and guilt, Albrecht goes to visit Giselle's grave, where he is surrounded by Wilis, spirits of maidens who have died as a result of being betrayed by faithless lovers. Hilarion comes to Giselle's grave but is surrounded by Wilis. The Queen shows no mercy and commands the Wilis to throw him into a nearby lake. Albrecht is condemned to the same fate, but Giselle warns him. The Queen, wanting revenge, commands Albrecht to dance. He is drawn toward his beloved and dances until he is exhausted. Giselle sustains him until dawn breaks. The daylight destroys the Wilis' power, and he is saved though Giselle must now return to her grave forever.

when they get to the mad scene they're not surprised? They've seen beforehand that she's passionate, she's on the brink." Every gesture, from the way Giselle looks at Albrecht to the way she touches the petals of a flower, must reveal that Giselle is a fragile young woman whose capacity for deep emotion puts her on the edge of madness.

Giselle goes mad and dies at the end of Act I. In the second half of the ballet, she's a ghost. How does a ballerina transform herself from a crazed, grief-stricken girl to a supernatural creature?

It's all done during the intermission. First the dancer changes her hairstyle and costume; from Giselle's peasant dress she slips into the translucent white gown and wings of the Wilis. Then she powders her body all over so that her skin glows ghostly white.

Some dancers slam their pointe shoes against a hard surface until they are as soft as bedroom slippers. This makes them harder to dance in, because there is very little support left, but they won't make a noise against the floor, so the ballerina can make her steps as soft as a spirit's. This kind of careful dancing demands huge stamina and control. Even when she's walking, the dancer must look as if she is scarcely skimming the ground. (It also helps to have a terrific partner who will make sure that your feet rarely touch the floor!)

Finally there is the critical mental transformation. The dancer imagines that she is no longer human but a spirit without bones or blood, as weightless and fleeting as a breeze. If the spectators don't believe in this transformation, they will soon be yawning in their seats. But if the performance is convincing, the audience will be drawn into the story and transported to another world.

Melody Masters

It took Adolphe Adam slightly more than one week to compose the music for *Giselle*, a score that many dancers find pretty, if a bit soupy. (Nikolaj Hübbe says it may work in the theater, but it's not something you'd buy to listen to at home.) Yet the great Tchaikovsky himself considered it to be a model of perfect ballet music, and he studied Adam's work again and again when he composed his own ballets.

Adam (who also composed the Christmas carol "O Holy Night") was one of the first composers to use leitmotifs — melodies attached to certain characters that are repeated whenever that character appears. Tchaikovsky also tended to recycle his melodies. Once he had a good tune in his head, he loved to repeat it.

Occasionally a dancer is chosen by a choreographer to have a work especially created to suit his or her own strengths and personality. *Giselle* was created for Carlotta Grisi (one of the choreographers, Jules Perrot, was her husband and teacher) to highlight her light, airy dancing.

Everything Old Is New Again

There are two kinds of choreology — the written record of dance movements. Labanotation is written as if the movements were being viewed from above; it is used to record many kinds of movement, not just dance. Benesh Notation, used by most ballet companies, looks similar to a musical score, with little stick figures placed on a staff; it is written as if the movement was being viewed from behind.

The *Giselle* we see today is not exactly the same as the one that first appeared in Paris 150 years ago. As they are passed down from one generation of dancers to another, ballets are constantly revised and restaged. Over the years, for example, the male roles in most ballets have been expanded to give men more solo parts.

Even the stories can be changed. Sometimes these changes are fairly small. In *The Nutcracker*, for example, Clara may be called Mary, and she may be transported to the world of ballet instead of the land of sweets, or she may even become the Sugarplum Fairy. Cinderella may have stepbrothers as well as stepsisters. In *Swan Lake*, Siegfried's mother may be conspiring with Von Rothbart to destroy Siegfried's love for Odette.

But sometimes the changes to the ballet are much more profound, with the choreographer retaining only the music and the core idea of the original ballet. Imagine a *Swan Lake* danced only by men, or, *The Sleeping Beauty*'s Princess Aurora as a rebellious modern-day street kid. Or Giselle in a lunatic asylum, with the Wilis dressed as patients in hospital gowns.

Sound like good ideas? Not to some. "If they want to do these things, let them do a new ballet!" says artistic director Celia Franca. Others say that if dance doesn't change, it will soon be about as interesting as an old shoe.

Choreographer George Balanchine discusses a sketch with costume designer Barbara Karinska

Gregory Osborne of the Universal Ballet as Albrecht

Albrecht:
Heartless Flirt or True Love?

To prepare for the part of Albrecht, dancers must first decide what they think of him. We know that he loves Giselle by the end of the ballet, but what about at the beginning?

"The more I analyze it, the more I start hating Albrecht. He just went down to the village for a little hanky-panky and used poor Giselle to have a good time."

— Ivan Nagy

"He was truly in love with her from the beginning. He had visited her often in the village and just didn't think for one minute what the consequences would be."

— Nikolaj Hübbe

How Do Dancers Learn All Those Steps?

How does a dancer learn a ballet? Not only are the steps themselves exacting and intricate, but everyone must be in precisely the right place at the right time. In a complicated pas de deux, with daring lifts and turns, one second's hesitation can mean disaster.

Dancers need to learn and memorize their parts quickly and perfectly, and some are better at this than others. It's said that Rudolf Nureyev learned his roles so quickly, he only had to see a dance to remember it. And for her first season with the Bolshoi, ballerina Maya Plisetskaya mastered no less than nine major roles.

Today's dancers use videotape and film as well as choreology — written scores for ballets — to help them learn their parts. But traditionally this knowledge has been passed down from generation to generation by the dancers themselves. Experienced dancers not only teach the steps, they explain the mood and feeling of the steps, and can demonstrate how to do them more effectively. For a young dancer there is no greater honor or thrill than to be taught a part by a world-class dancer, and no better way to establish a link to a whole generation of dancers who have struggled to master the very same role.

How Are Ballets Born?

Choreographers, the people who make up the steps to go with the music, usually create their ballets by using dancers as live models. The dancers are instructed to try different moves so that the choreographer can determine what does and does not work, before deciding on the final sequence. That is why a ballet is said to be made *on* a dancer. The dancer is like a living piece of clay set in motion, and the choreographer is the sculptor.

This means that choreographing a new ballet, even a very short one, can be extremely costly. The dancers, rehearsal time and studio rental must all be paid for, and that doesn't even include the costumes, sets, lighting, stage time and musicians. Choreographers say they feel a huge amount of pressure when they walk into a room to compose a ballet. Opening night may already have been announced, the studio is filled with dancers, limbered up and ready, and assistants, video cameras and choreologists are set to record every move. Everyone waits expectantly as, minute by minute, this expensive session ticks away. And the ballet may still be little more than ideas in the choreographer's head. George Balanchine, the great American choreographer, was known to create the beginning and ending of a ballet first, and then fill in the middle. He also found inspiration in unexpected ways. During one session, a dancer tripped and fell as she ran from the stage. Balanchine, liking what he saw, ended up adding the movement to the final ballet.

George Balanchine rehearses
with ballerina Maria Tallchief

Coppélia

Men Take Center Stage

In *La Sylphide*, James inadvertently causes the death of his true love. In *Giselle*, a frail girl goes mad and dies when her lover betrays her. By the middle of the nineteenth century, ballets were, admittedly, becoming a tad gloomy.

Then came *Coppélia*, a story about regular folks. No more fairies or medieval princes but instead just some high-spirited young people with a taste for partying and mischief. Most of all, *Coppélia* had a sense of humor.

The dancers soon learned that playing comedy can be much more challenging than playing drama. As Claude Bessy says, "It is more difficult to make someone laugh than cry." You need perfect timing, otherwise a hilarious moment can easily turn ridiculous.

And there are plenty of potentially ridiculous moments in *Coppélia*. Swanilda asks an ear of wheat to tell her whether her boyfriend, Franz, truly loves her. Dr. Coppelius thinks he can turn a doll into a human being and is duped by Swanilda into believing he actually has. Franz sleeps for most of the second

The National Ballet of Canada's Martine Lamy as Dr. Coppelius's beloved doll

The great Danish dancer Erik Bruhn was famous for his bittersweet portrayal of Dr. Coppelius

half of the ballet, only to wake up and begin leaping over tables while Dr. Coppelius chases him around the room. (One dancer actually fell asleep during this scene, only to be jolted awake when one of his legs suddenly slipped off the table. And it is so difficult to burst into action after being still for so long that Danish dancer Erik Bruhn had an electric blanket added to the prop list so he could keep his muscles limber during his onstage "snooze.")

At first glance *Coppélia* seems to be little more than a bit of light fluff, but in fact the ballet is considerably more complicated. Dancers must pump out energy and enthusiasm from start to finish. And, unlike other story ballets that center on two young people in love, at the heart of *Coppélia* is the strange and somewhat puzzling character of old Dr. Coppelius, the inventor who tries to make the doll he loves come to life. Many dancers and critics say that Erik Bruhn was the best Dr. Coppelius ever. Bruhn's gifted acting made the audience pity old Dr. Coppelius, even while they were laughing at him.

Bruhn's performances in *Coppélia* came near the end of a career that changed the way the world viewed the male dancer. Along with famed Russian star Rudolf Nureyev, Bruhn helped raise the technical standard for male dancers. He also made audiences see that the male dancer's role was just as important as the ballerina's.

Although ballet began as a court entertainment performed by men, the ballerina soon found herself pushed to center stage when the pointe shoe made its appearance in the late eighteenth century. Male dancers simply could not compete. Men did try to dance on pointe for a while, but to no avail. Soon they were relegated to the role of porter — lifting and carrying the ballerina around the

Rudolf Nureyev wearing his trademark toque. He was constantly concerned about being exposed to drafts in air-conditioned theaters, and he often wore a hat or scarf during rehearsals.

Clockwise from top left: Edward Villella, Frank Augustyn, Raymond Smith and Rex Harrington. Male dancers are once again taking center stage.

Coppélia: Synopsis

Act I, Scene I

In the mid-nineteenth century in a small town on the border of Galicia, Franz and Swanilda are engaged to be married, though Swanilda suspects that Franz is enamored of Coppélia, a beautiful girl who spends her days reading in the window of her father's workshop. The burgomaster gives Swanilda a sheaf of wheat that, according to legend, will reveal one's true love. But when she shakes it, the wheat is silent and she runs off in a huff.

That night, the village boys are teasing the strange old Dr. Coppelius. In the scuffle, his key falls to the ground. Swanilda finds it and sneaks into his workshop. Meanwhile, Franz climbs through an open window in search of his beloved Coppélia.

Act I, Scene II

Swanilda discovers that Coppélia is nothing but a life-size doll. When she hears Dr. Coppelius returning, she quickly puts on Coppélia's clothes and takes the doll's place.

Franz is discovered by Dr. Coppelius, who gives him drugged wine that puts him to sleep. The old doctor then tries to transfer Franz's life force to his beloved doll. To amuse him, Swanilda pretends to be the doll and does everything he asks her to do. Soon she tires of the game and reveals her deception. Dr. Coppelius is brokenhearted.

Franz awakens and is reunited with his true love, Swanilda.

Act II

Swanilda and Franz are married while the citizens dance in celebration. The festivities include a betrothal waltz, and dances depicting dawn and prayer. Dr. Coppelius is paid for the damage to his workshop.

stage. Not many men wanted to spend their careers carting ballerinas around (and not all of them are as light as a feather!) and before long there was such a shortage of male dancers that women were forced to dance the male roles. In fact, the opening performance of *Coppélia* had a ballerina dancing the role of Franz because no male dancers were available.

The heyday of the ballerina lasted through the end of the nineteenth century with the creation of the Tchaikovsky ballet classics like *Swan Lake* and *The Nutcracker*. Yet slowly but surely men came back to dominate ballet.

Martine Lamy portrays
a life-sized doll

As early as 1832, for example, when Maria Taglioni was dazzling audiences with her nimble pointe work, the Danish dancer and choreographer Auguste Bournonville decided to change the choreography of *La Sylphide* to showcase his own athletic dancing. Bournonville choreographed a male role full of bounding leaps and turns that required the dancer to be as strong and agile as a track star. (He was also a bit of a stage hog and made sure that the ballerina's solos ended with her running off into the wings, while the male solos ended with a grand flourish onstage — this was to make sure that he got the applause and she didn't.)

Over the years, most of the classic ballets have been revised to include increasingly difficult roles for men. Male dancers are now under constant pressure to become stronger and faster. Dance schools routinely include weight training for their male students, and it's been proven that ballet is more physically demanding than sports like football and hockey. Higher jumps! More turns! Faster leaps! Some wonder whether focusing on these feats is turning ballet into an athletic contest instead of an art.

Dancer Faints... from Standing Still!

In *Coppélia*, dancers play the life-size dolls in Dr. Coppelius' workshop, and in certain scenes they are required to stand perfectly still, for long periods of time. Standing motionless under hot lights, in cumbersome costumes, is harder than it seems. During one performance, a dancer actually keeled over in a dead faint halfway through the second act!

What Do Guys Really Wear under Their Tights?

Male dancers wear a dance belt — like reinforced underwear — under their tights. The belt is not terribly comfortable, but it improves the line of the legs and is needed for protection and support during all those leaps and bounds.

Susan Jaffe and Fernando Bujones in the 1991 production of the American Ballet Theater's production of *Coppélia*

Mikhail Baryshnikov

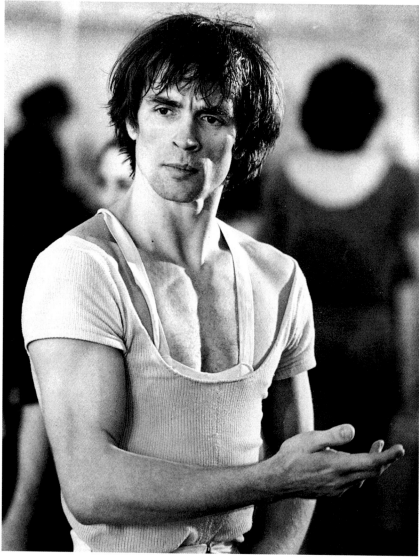

Rudolf Nureyev

But a new generation of male dancers has risen to this challenge. They are strong, driven, athletic and graceful. Like today's championship figure skaters, young ballet stars like Carlos Acosta are pushing the envelope, creating new steps and spectacular jumps that highlight their talents, and make the rest of the world's dancers sit up and take notice.

Vaslav Nijinsky

The male dancer's changing role has also meant a change in body type over the years. This transition can be seen in the three male Russian stars who have been largely responsible for bringing ballet to the mass public: the delicate grace of Vaslav Nijinsky, the tigerlike power of Rudolf Nureyev, the lean energy of Mikhail Baryshnikov.

Others are paying attention as well. In ancient Greece, young soldiers considered dance to be an essential part of their military training, because it taught them how to carry themselves properly and discipline their bodies. Many of today's athletes have recognized that they, too, can benefit from ballet. Gymnasts, swimmers and skaters often take supplementary ballet training, and even hockey and football coaches have been known to send their players to dance class in order to improve their coordination, balance, flexibility and strength.

Today's ballet audiences are as intrigued by the male dancers as they are by the ballerinas. This interest has even filtered down to ballet schools, where directors now say that the prospects for boys are very exciting. "There may be more talent in the schools among the boys than the girls," says the Royal Ballet's Monica Mason.

As fit as athletes, as respected as artists, as glamorous as movie stars — today the male dancer has definitely recovered the spotlight.

The Kid in the Tights

Like many male dancers, Edward Villella, a star with the New York City Ballet, came into ballet by accident. He grew up in the tough New York City neighborhood of Queens ("Not too many guys in Queens wearing tights," as he says), where boys were more interested in playing baseball in the street than going to dance class. After being hit by a ball one day, Edward was forced to accompany his mother to watch his sister's ballet class. Self-conscious at being stared at by a room full of girls, he slipped around to the back of the class and started jumping and goofing around. The teacher told him that if he wanted to join the class, he must do it properly; the next day, Villella showed up for class in tights.

It wasn't easy telling his buddies that he was a dancer, but ballet training made him fast and strong, and he was easily able to defend himself against the teasing!

Edward Villella proved that there was nothing sissy about ballet. He was once featured in *Life* magazine under the headline: "Is This Man the Country's Best Athlete?"

The Nutcracker

Celebrating the Ballet Family

A Christmas party in a fabulous mansion, toys that come to life, dancing flowers and snowflakes, a magical kingdom of sweets. *The Nutcracker*, that luscious holiday confection, has become the most widely performed ballet in the world.

Yet many dancers hate it. This is partly because it is performed so often ("By every ballet school and company in every town in the land," mutters one cranky dancer), but it is also because the dancers dislike the weak story and the superficial and static characters. After a few productions, *The Nutcracker* can feel like little more than a sugary showpiece designed to make money off festive-minded audiences during the Christmas season. "It's half a kilo of makeup and then get on with it," says Ivan Nagy.

But *The Nutcracker* is also a celebration, and its sense of wonder and glorious music can soften the heart of the surliest dancer who has performed the ballet hundreds of times.

Traditionally dancers learn how to apply makeup from experienced dancers. Some companies offer makeup classes, and the largest companies employ makeup artists.

Each costume must be fitted to the individual dancer, so that it can flow and move as the dancers dance. This costume designer is making some last-minute adjustments to a ballerina's costume as she waits in the wings to go onstage.

The Nutcracker requires the entire company to be on deck for the performance, from the most experienced veterans to the youngest stars of tomorrow. Juicy roles, such as that of the stern and mysterious Herr Drosselmeyer, are played by character dancers. These are usually senior dancers who act more than they arabesque, and they are the heart and soul of all the story ballets — Dr. Coppelius in *Coppélia*, Von Rothbart in *Swan Lake*, the wicked fairy Carabosse in *The Sleeping Beauty*.

Not all dancers welcome the thought of performing these character parts. To some it's considered a sign of being washed up — too old to dance principal roles like the Sugarplum Fairy and the Nutcracker Prince. Yet character dancers are the backbone of a company, passing on their stage experience and acting skills to the younger dancers, while finding new ways to express themselves on stage. And character dancers have fun; they have the freedom to make their performance a little bit different every night, by changing the direction of a look, an expression, or their makeup.

The Nutcracker also showcases the corps de ballet, dancers who perform as a group. In some ballets the corps act in large part as a chorus or background for the soloists, but corps dancing is one of the highlights of the *The Nutcracker*. When the ballet was first performed in Russia, even the wealthiest patrons requested seats in the upper balcony to better admire the complicated patterns that the corps would weave over the stage.

And the dances for the soloists, though they may not offer much in terms of dramatic depth, are beautiful and technically challenging — ranging from classical pas de deux to exotic divertissements that give the audience a glimpse of Russia, Arabia and China.

Maybe best of all, *The Nutcracker* is full of children — usually young dance students acquiring their first taste of the stage. Audiences and artistic directors often scan the ranks for signs of future stardom. Will this year's Clara be the prima ballerina of tomorrow? Will that third mouse from the left be the next Nureyev?

In fact, many of today's stars started out in just this way — on the bottom rung of the ballet ladder. From there, however, the path to stardom, even to a professional career, involves a combination of hard work, mettle, talent, the right body and sometimes sheer luck.

The Royal Winnipeg Ballet's corps de ballet performing in *The Nutcracker*

The entire cast of Canada's National Ballet company, including young ballet students, is on call during this performance of *The Nutcracker*

Many aspiring dancers begin intensive daily dance training at an early age (eight to ten for girls; boys may begin somewhat later) by attending a professional ballet school. But there is fierce competition for spots in these schools, and the selection process is thorough and tough. There is much more to being a ballet dancer than being able to do difficult steps perfectly (many schools actually prefer to take children with no previous training). Ballet dancers must be emotionally strong and quick learners. They must be musical, possess stage presence and have natural acting ability. And physically they must have the right build and proportions. This can be difficult to predict when a child is only eight to ten years old. School directors look closely at a child's bone structure, muscle tone, shoulders and neck. Directors like Claude Bessy look for good feet — "A boy's feet should not be too small. He must have a good platform for jumping and turning. Good feet are more important for boys than for girls." Some directors even like to meet the child's parents — to help them predict what kind of body the child may grow into as an adult!

The first act of the Alberta Ballet's production of *The Nutcracker*

After years of schooling, a lucky few are selected to join the corps de ballet. From there they eventually hope to become soloists and, after a great deal of hard work, principal dancers.

Sometimes, though this is very rare, a dancer can speed through the ranks. Paloma Herrera of the American Ballet Theater began training at age seven in her native Argentina. At the age of fifteen she moved to New York to study at the School of American Ballet. After a mere six months she was accepted into the corps de ballet. Two years later she was promoted to soloist, and then to principal dancer at the tender age of nineteen, yet Paloma sees her quick rise to the top as an opportunity to work even harder. "I think it's great because I have all this time to keep working and get better," she says.

Paloma Herrera dancing in a performance of *Don Quixote*

The Nutcracker: Synopsis

Act I, Scene I

At a grand family party on Christmas Eve, a magician, Herr Drosselmeyer, arrives and distributes presents to the children. Then, from two boxes step four life-size clockwork toys. The toys are wound up and begin to dance.

The boys attack the dolls and Clara begins to cry at their meanness. To make her happy, Herr Drosselmeyer gives her a nutcracker doll. But the mischievous Fritz is jealous and smashes it on the floor.

Clara is forlorn. That night she wakes up and creeps downstairs to fetch her new gift, only to discover that her Christmas tree has magically grown (or has she shrunk?), and the toys, including her precious nutcracker, have come to life. Clara witnesses a battle between the mice and toy soldiers, and she saves her nutcracker from the Mouse King.

The nutcracker turns into a handsome prince who invites her to accompany him on a journey.

Act I, Scene II

The travelers find themselves in the wondrous Land of Snowflakes. The Snow Queen appears and dances with the Prince.

Act II

Continuing on their journey, Clara and the Prince come to the Kingdom of Sweets, where the Sugarplum Fairy shows Clara some wonderful entertainment. Clara returns home just before morning, in time to wonder whether her nighttime adventures were all a dream.

Every member of the ballet family must work very hard to produce *The Nutcracker*. It is a madhouse to stage, though in the end this just adds to the excitement. The designers, armed with plump budgets, usually go to town with costumes, sets and

Mikhail Baryshnikov dances the part of the Nutcracker doll

special effects. The wings are crammed with dancers of all ages, many of them performing multiple roles (there can be more than one hundred dancers and almost twice as many costumes). There are sword fights and extravagant outfits that range from heavy mouse heads to giant ladies in huge hoopskirts that explode with children. (It's hot and stuffy waiting under that skirt to make your grand entrance — a good introduction to the ballet tradition of suffering for the sake of art!) And there are props galore — trees grow to gigantic heights, shoes are tossed about the stage, children dance with dolls and baby carriages, fake snow falls over the stage.

Travel the World — Go to the Ballet

Most full-length classical ballets include ensembles based on folk dances from around the world. You'll see a Polish mazurka in *Coppélia*, Chinese and Arabian dances in *The Nutcracker*, a Spanish bolero in *Swan Lake*.

Usually these divertissements have very little to do with the story, though they do add a dash of exoticism and atmosphere. They serve as a reminder that classical ballets were originally created to entertain audiences who had little knowledge of the world outside their own cities and cultures. Travel was expensive, there were no films, there was no television or radio, and even illustrated books were rare and costly. Watching a Spanish bolero, with its colorful costumes and exotic music, was the next best thing to traveling to Spain oneself.

And then there's Tchaikovsky's music, as rich and delicious as a sugarplum itself.

It's impossible to overestimate just how important music is to the dancer. Most dancers say that it was the need to move to music that drew them to ballet in the first place. "Music first, then movement," says Fernando Bujones. Music is the heartbeat of movement, and Tchaikovsky's score for *The Nutcracker* will inspire any dancer to give his body and soul, no matter how tacky the production, how ridiculous the story.

"It never fails me when I hear that score and I see that tree going up," admits Anthony Dowell.

Not Just Kid's Stuff

Today, songwriters, film-makers and Broadway producers recycle fairy tales for popular entertainment. *The Little Mermaid, Beauty and the Beast* and *Aladdin* are all ancient tales that have been dusted off and restaged for young audiences.

Ballet composers and choreographers did the very same thing one hundred years ago. *Giselle, The Sleeping Beauty, Cinderella* and *The Firebird* are all either old fairy tales or legends that have been

The Mouse King and the Nutcracker face off in the first act of the Alberta Ballet Company's production of *The Nutcracker*

put to music and dance. In the nineteenth century they were considered sophisticated adult fare and presented in opulent opera houses and theaters.

Why did choreographers choose nursery stories for their ballets? One of the reasons fairy tales have endured is because they contain all the elements of a good story. Handsome heroes and heroines to admire, evil villains to fear, misfortune, happy endings and sometimes even a magic sorcerer or two, just to keep things interesting.

No audience, young or old, can resist such a combination.

The Partner in the Pit

Most conductors know the special hazards involved in directing a
ballet orchestra — dancers pirouetting themselves right off
the stage and onto the musicians' laps, dodging daggers that
accidentally fly into the orchestra pit during the fight scenes of
Romeo and Juliet (though sometimes the pit is covered with a
net to keep the musicians protected from soaring projectiles).
The conductor is the dancer's invisible partner, but this marriage
is not always an easy one. That's because the dancer and the
conductor can't always agree on who is boss. Should the music
run the dance, or should the dance run the music?

Some conductors feel that being faithful to the music is
paramount. They will simply follow the score, and tough luck for
the dancer who can't keep up. "There have been a couple of

"My biggest job is drawing the
orchestra into the performance.
They're in the pit and they can't
see. … I try to convey my
enthusiasm or accent the
emotional moments in order to
make a connection between the
pit and the stage. The orchestra
has to feel as important as the
dancers." — Ormsby Wilkins,
Music Director and Principal
Conductor of The National Ballet
Orchestra

Because ballet is such a physically demanding art form, students begin training at a very young age. Here, young ballet students practice at the barre at a ballet school in Budapest, Hungary.

occasions when I could have hung one or two conductors," says Fernando Bujones. "It wasn't that they weren't talented. It's just that they had a bigger ego than baton." Other dancers agree. "The conductor can kill you," says Natalya Makarova.

Sensitive conductors, on the other hand, are heroes to a dancer. They have one eye on the stage at all times and will gently slow down the musicians to let a dancer complete and hold an arabesque. They know that male dancers who are taller or heavier than average need more time to make their leaps. Ormsby Wilkins, who has conducted ballet orchestras all over the world says, "You have to be sympathetic if a dancer is having a rough day, or performing the role for the first time ... you have to help the dancer ... still maintaining the integrity of the music."

Caution: Costume May Be Hazardous

A good wardrobe staff balances appearance with safety and security. Costumes must stand up to hours of being pulled and stretched under hot lights. Karen Kain remembers a small gray wigpiece flying off her head in the middle of a performance and landing on the floor, where it looked exactly like a mouse and caused no end of consternation among the corps. On another occasion, the hook and eye holding the back of a ballerina's costume became entangled in her partner's sleeve while she was doing a pirouette. There was no choice but to keep on spinning and let the costume rip. After all, the show must go on.

Making a tutu in the wardrobe department at the National Ballet of Canada

Ballerina Slides into Orchestra Pit!

A good dance floor has to have some give so that the dancers don't injure themselves landing those big leaps. Dancers accept that every stage surface will be different, but sometimes the floor can be downright dangerous. Every dancer will have horror stories about the time they had to dance on concrete or freshly waxed linoleum. And in Europe and South America, many theater stages are raked — slightly tilted toward the front to give the audience a better view. A raked stage can make jumps look higher, but dancers may have to put on the brakes in a hurry to stop themselves from sliding right into the orchestra pit. "It's like dancing on a hill," says Edward Villella. "Your balance is odd. Ballerinas would pull me off my feet just by offering me a hand … it drove me nuts."

The Sleeping Beauty

The Push for Perfection

The role of Aurora in *The Sleeping Beauty* is considered the Mount Everest of every ballerina's career. Because the role is so technically difficult, it is one of the last a classical ballerina will add to her repertoire. It is also one of the first roles she will drop, since she must be at the peak of her physical conditioning just to get through it.

It was Marius Petipa, head of the Imperial Ballet of Russia, who was responsible for this torture test of technique and stamina. Like his other celebrated ballets, *The Nutcracker* and *Swan Lake*, *The Sleeping Beauty* was created in late nineteenth-century Russia, home of the richest court in Europe. Though the tsarist regime was filled with corruption and injustice, it was a good place for ballet. The tsar directly employed only the very best choreographers and dancers, and gave them the money, staff and freedom to do whatever they wanted. Geniuses like Peter Ilyich Tchaikovsky were commissioned to write ballet music, and

Marius Petipa (1818–1910), the French-born dancer/ choreographer, was one of the most important builders of the Imperial Ballet of Russia

The Royal Ballet's 1989 production of *The Sleeping Beauty*

Corps member Brenda Little of The National Ballet of Canada stretches at the barre before a class

masters like Marius Petipa were lured from France to create dazzling entertainment for the Russian court. With *The Sleeping Beauty*, Petipa outdid himself. This ballet is a marathon of one magnificent dance showpiece after another.

Dancers still curse Petipa for putting in so many tricks and balletic tours de force, such as the Rose Adagio and the Blue Bird pas de deux, at the expense of developing the story and characters. But they all want to perform this "circus" ballet, precisely because it is such a challenge. Ballet dancers are like that. As Claude Bessy says, "If it were easy, nobody would want to do it."

After a performance of *The Sleeping Beauty*, a dancer is a physical wreck. When the final curtain comes down, stage smiles collapse into grimaces of pain, as the prince and princess hobble into the wings, gasping for breath. As the ballerina peels off her blood-soaked tights and sticks her swollen, blistered feet in a bucket of ice water, she wonders how she ever made it to the end, and how she can possibly ever make it through again.

But she does, because strain, pain and the ability not to show it are all part of the art.

Ballet is hard. And it's getting harder. There is an increased focus on technical ability, as dancers push their bodies to jump higher, turn faster, stretch farther. Like skaters, gymnasts and other athletes, dancers face technical requirements that become more punishing year after year. In the early days a dancer might have done only a half-dozen pirouettes during an entire performance, and ballerinas would have spent very little time on pointe. Even thirty years ago, ballet was technically less difficult than it is now. (Merrill Ashley once said that when she joined the New York City Ballet in 1967, she couldn't even do a double pirouette — a step that most intermediate ballet students can master today.)

Dancers need stamina — not only physical stamina, but mental stamina as well. Yet, at the same time that dancers are required to keep their bodies at the peak of physical conditioning, they are also encouraged to look a certain way. A slender ballerina (as opposed to a thicker, muscular one) looks better in a tutu, is easier to lift and blends into the lines of the corps. And the hard truth is that no matter how talented and strong you are, if you don't *look* like a dancer, you probably won't be hired by a classical ballet company. "You're probably out on your ear," says Margot Lehman, a past president of the American Dance Guild. "Nobody wants a little tubby."

Ballerinas are expected to have perfect bodies. They should be as wispy as the airy creatures they portray. The dance world is full of stories about dancers who have gone to extreme and unhealthy lengths to stay thin: the dancer who ate nothing but jujubes and sesame snaps; the ballerina who dropped dead from a suspected eating disorder. A surprising number of dancers smoke, and just about every dancer has been on a diet at one time or another.

Ballet companies and schools are becoming increasingly aware of this problem, and they watch closely for signs of eating disorders such as anorexia nervosa. Larger companies can afford to employ professional dieticians, nutritionists and psychologists to counsel dancers and watch for the danger signs, because being too thin compromises a dancer's health, both physically and mentally. Not

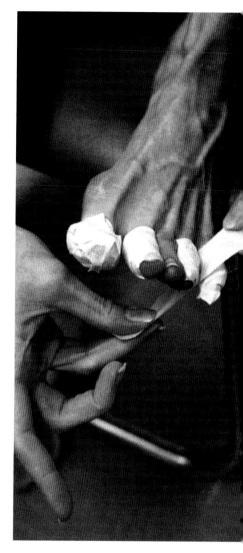

This dancer uses tape to cover the blisters and welts that dancing on pointe creates

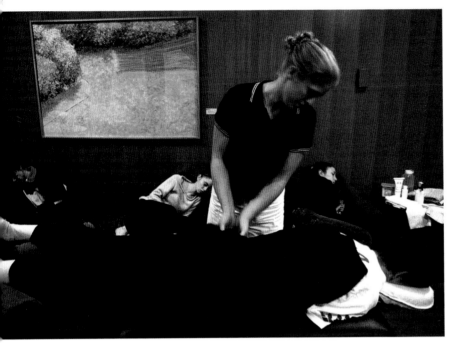

Physical therapy is a day-to-day part of a dancer's life. This is a typical behind-the-scenes look at a dance company. One dancer receives a massage, while in the background other members of the troupe catch some much needed sleep.

only must a dancer maintain great strength and stamina, a ballerina who is too thin will have more difficulty recovering from injuries, stress and fatigue — things all dancers face every single day.

Ballet involves more than the physical stress of daily classes, rehearsals and performances. Some years there are months of being on tour, perhaps in a different country, trying to keep body and mind in top shape while living out of a suitcase and sleeping in strange hotels. Free time is rare, and even then there are shoe ribbons to sew on, feet to soak, tights and leotards to wash, muscles to massage, sleep to catch up on.

It can be a lonely, hard life, and you can't count on financial reward. Dancers are generally poorly paid and have little job security. "You have to be prepared to work really hard and not make very much money. You have to love it a lot," says Karen Kain. Many dancers travel long distances to find jobs. They are often forced to adjust to a new country, a new language and new friends — all while living far away from family. For women, a dance career may mean postponing or possibly abandoning the thought of having children.

Dancers are also extremely hard on their bodies. Injury is commonplace in ballet, whether it's accidental (coming down badly off a leap) or chronic (simply the wear and tear of years of daily training). The staff roster of a large ballet company can sometimes look like a list of hospital personnel. There are usually several doctors on the list, including a few surgeons, podiatrists, physiotherapists, massage therapists, sports medicine specialists and chiropractors. At any given time, at least half the dancers in a company are likely to be receiving treatment for a dance-related injury of some kind, and some spend many years battling chronic pain. Before retiring after a long, illustrious career, Merrill Ashley was spending more time treating her injuries (sometimes six hours a day with a physical therapist) than she was dancing. And all dancers live in fear of the one injury that could end their careers for good.

Even if they stay healthy, dancers' careers are short. Some go on to become teachers, choreographers, artistic directors, choreologists and character dancers. But there are only a limited number of these opportunities, and it can be difficult to prepare for a new career. Ballet is so demanding it requires every ounce of energy and focus a dancer has. Most dancers have devoted their lives to dance since they were children.

Natalia Makarova rehearsing the American Ballet Theater's 1981 production of *Don Quixote*

Throughout the world there are now programs available to help dancers make successful career transitions once their dancing days are over. Dancers themselves are becoming increasingly aware that a dance career can be short, and they are making efforts to put backup plans in place. Jennifer Gelfand, for example, a star with the

Boston Ballet, who is only in her late twenties, combines dance with a burgeoning real-estate career.

Then again, there are some stars who have danced marvelously into their forties and fifties, including Margot Fonteyn, Galina Ulanova, Natalia Makarova and Mikhail Baryshnikov. The hard reality remains, however, that only a few

The Sleeping Beauty: Synopsis

Prologue

All the fairies of the kingdom have been invited to the palace for the christening of the Princess Aurora, with the exception of the evil fairy, Carabosse. Furious at this insult, Carabosse arrives anyway and condemns Aurora to prick her finger and die on her sixteenth birthday. Luckily, the good Lilac Fairy is able to erase part of Carabosse's fairy magic. The princess will not die but sleep, she says, until she is awakened by the kiss of a prince.

Act I

When the day of her sixteenth birthday party arrives, Aurora is wooed by four suitors in the palace garden. Carabosse, disguised as an old woman, arrives at the celebration and gives Aurora a bouquet of flowers in which a spindle is concealed.

Aurora pricks her finger on the sharp spindle and collapses. Guided by the Lilac Fairy, Aurora is carried into the palace by the courtiers. There the Lilac Fairy casts a spell over the court, causing everyone to fall asleep and a thick forest to grow around the palace.

Act II, Scene I

One hundred years later, Prince Florimund and his courtiers are in the forest hunting for deer. He becomes melancholic and sends everyone away so that he may be alone. In his solitude, he is visited by the Lilac Fairy, who learns that he is looking for love. She tells him of an enchanted palace and the sleeping princess who lies there. A beautiful vision of Princess Aurora appears before him. He falls in love and boards a magical boat to search for her.

Act II, Scene II

Carabosse, now old and gray, continues to spin her wicked web. With the arrival of Prince Florimund, she finally collapses, overpowered by goodness and virtue.

Inside the palace, Prince Florimund comes upon the sleeping Aurora and, recognizing his true love, kisses her. Magically, she awakens and the entire court is restored to its earlier splendor.

Act III

The scene opens with a magnificent royal wedding in the palace ballroom. Dances by various storybook characters, including Puss in Boots, Blue Bird, and Red Riding Hood and the Wolf, are performed. Descending the grand staircase, Princess Aurora and Prince Florimund arrive and declare their love.

can dance beyond the age of forty. (At the Paris Opera Ballet, retired dancers receive a good pension, but retirement from dance is compulsory. For women, retirement comes the day they turn forty; for men it's forty-four. No exceptions.)

So why do they do it? Are they crazy? Maybe a little. The kind of dedication required for something as difficult as ballet requires a certain amount of strangeness. Yet dancers and performers everywhere share a love for the stage and for the thrill of live applause after a perfect performance. In the end, it is that applause that makes all the hard work worthwhile.

The Rose Adagio in the American Ballet Theater's 1987 production of *The Sleeping Beauty*

However, even looking back over a career filled with injuries and sacrifice, most dancers simply cannot imagine doing anything else with their lives. "It's a very difficult life, but if I could, I would start again," says Natalia Makarova.

The Rose Adagio

Along with the thirty-two fouettés in *Swan Lake*, the Rose Adagio is the ballerina's biggest test of skill and nerve. It comes shortly after Princess Aurora's initial entrance, when she is barely used to being on stage. While standing on one pointe, with her other leg behind her in a high attitude (an extremely difficult position to hold), the ballerina is slowly pivoted by four dancers in turn (Aurora's four suitors). At the end of each turn, she lets go of the suitor's hand and holds a long balance.

It's ridiculously difficult. The body must be held absolutely still. The attitude leg must not drop even a fraction of an inch.

If I Could Just Take a Wee Nap

A dancer's life is exhausting. Karen Kain admits that she has fallen asleep while lying on stage as Aurora, in front of an audience of three thousand people at the Metropolitan Opera House in New York!

Margaret Illman as Princess Aurora dances the Rose Adagio

And the musical buildup is almost excruciating — like performing to a drumroll. "If [the balances] don't go the way I want them to go," says Amanda McKerrow, "I feel like I've not only let myself down, I've let the music down, too."

Few dancers can completely hide the immense strain of these balances. The ballerina's hand trembles slightly, and her eyes are fixed with steely determination while the audience collectively holds its breath. The Rose Adagio is classical ballet's most dramatic example of perfect balance and strength — to say nothing of sheer will — at work.

A Team Effort

Many critics (including the composer himself) consider *The Sleeping Beauty* to be Peter Ilyich Tchaikovsky's finest ballet. This is a particularly stunning achievement, considering how the music was composed. Although traditionally choreographers create dances to fit existing music, in this case Marius Petipa wanted no such restrictions. He choreographed the ballet using small figurines and then gave Tchaikovsky a written description of the music. He specified exactly what he wanted, right down to the mood and timing for virtually every second of music.

Here are Petipa's instructions for the scene where Aurora pricks her finger:

Suddenly, Aurora notices the old woman who beats on her knitting needles a 2/4 measure. Gradually she changes to a very melodious waltz in 3/4, but then, suddenly a rest. Aurora pricks her finger, screams, pain. Blood streams — give eight measures in 4/4 wide. She begins to dance — dizziness — complete horror. It is frenzy. As if bitten by a tarantula, she keeps turning and then falls unexpectedly. ... This must last from 24 to 32 measures. At the end there should be a tremolo of a few measures, as if shouts of pain and sobs. Father, mother!

When he finally completed his first draft in 1889, Tchaikovsky wrote simply, "Thank God!" When he finished orchestrating the music three months later, he said he felt as if "a whole mountain has fallen off my shoulders."

Ballet Makes Ballerina Sick!

Ballet dancers love what they do, but that doesn't mean it comes easily. Some dancers can't sleep a wink the night before a show. Others get so nervous that they are overcome with stomachaches, nausea, dry mouth and even vomiting before a performance.

Experts say pre-performance jitters can be a good thing. It can give a performance excitement and flair. It is also nature's way of reducing the chance of injury by bringing the body to a peak of energy and readiness.

Peter Ilyich Tchaikovsky (1840–93) as a young man

Welcome … to the House of Pain

Sometimes it seems as though ballet was invented simply to torture every single part of the body.

Hips

Ballet dancers are constantly trying to increase their turnout — pushing their legs to rotate outward within the hip socket.

Back

Impossible back bends, high arabesques, to say nothing of the lifting required by the male dancer. All are very hard on the lower back.

Knees

Every time a dancer comes down from a jump, the knees absorb the shock. Other steps require the bottom part of the leg to rotate within the knee joint. This movement does not come naturally.

Head

Those sleek, perfectly secure buns aren't easy to achieve. A dancer's hair is pulled, sprayed, twisted and stuck with elastics, nets, pins, tiaras and hairpieces. Short hairstyles are discouraged.

Feet

You have only to look at a dancer's bare feet to see that the word torture is not an exaggeration: misshapen, callused, blistered, bleeding, blackened nails, enlarged toe joints, feet so swollen that they won't fit in their shoes.

Neck

Dancers are taught how to "spot" so they don't become dizzy during turns. They focus on one place, hold it in their sight as long as possible and then whip the head around to spot it once again. That whipping motion puts tremendous strain on the neck.

Now That You're a Famous Dancer, You Can … Go to Class

The basis for every dancer's conditioning, regardless of whether they are young students or prima ballerinas, is the daily class or training session. All dancers go through the same sequence of exercises, starting with slow pliés at the barre and building up through tendus and développés to adage work in the center and finally quick steps and jumps.

Every company class in every studio in the world looks and sounds the same: dancers in frayed, grungy rehearsal clothes, usually wearing their oldest, most tattered shoes; the sound of the pianist's music echoing tinnily in the big room; soles squeaking as feet press and slide across the floor; the gravelly crunch of shoes in the rosin box; the teacher calling out instructions in French, counting beats, snapping fingers, giving dancers corrections as they go through the same exercises they've been doing since they were children.

It might sound like a recipe for boredom and irritation, facing day after day of class, even after becoming a professional, but it isn't. For dancers, ballet class is like water. It sustains them. On stage you see the gracious smiles of dancers as they give the appearance of going through their moves with no effort. In class, however, you see eyes full of steely determination and intense concentration as they critically check their positions in the mirror. Each day the dancers try to hold a balance a second longer, stretch a leg a fraction of an inch farther, come down from a jump just a little more softly, make that turn just a bit faster.

Professional dancers say, "If you miss class for one day, you know it. If you skip class for two days, the rest of the company knows it. If you miss it for three days, the whole world knows it."

Swan Lake

Dancing with Feeling

Ask any person on the street to name a ballet, and the most common answer will probably be *Swan Lake*. Even those who have never seen it think *Swan Lake* represents everything classical ballet is about. Dancers dressed in white, gliding across the stage in perfect rows. A soft, misty background. A handsome prince. Violins playing high, plaintive notes. Sadness and beauty.

Swan Lake is the most popular ballet in the world. And, unlike *The Nutcracker*, it is a favorite with audiences and dancers alike.

Why are dancers so drawn to this ballet? Why does a dancer know that once she has mastered the dual role of Odette/Odile, she can truly call herself a ballerina?

It's true that *Swan Lake* is one of the most difficult ballets to perform. Even the corps de ballet must be absolutely perfect. The choreography is so slow and precise that one foot, head or tutu out of line will clearly leap out at the audience. Dancers must have enormous control and concentration. (The seemingly simple "down" position, where the swans sit with their heads bent over their legs, for example, is a painfully difficult one to

The four cygnets dance in perfect formation in the National Ballet of Canada's production of *Swan Lake*

A New York City Ballet rehearsal of *Swan Lake*, with Suzanne Farrell and Jacques d'Amboise

Johann Persson as the prince in a National Ballet of Canada performance of *Swan Lake*

A ballerina must make a quick transformation, both mentally and physically, from the good Odette into the evil Odile. Here Greta Hodgkinson appears as Odile.

achieve and hold, let alone get up from gracefully!) And that famous charming dance with the four cygnets is also much harder than it looks. One tiny slip of the foot and all four swans can go down like a row of dominoes.

But *Swan Lake* offers more than a technical challenge. Dancers want to do more than simply master the steps. They want to *feel* something when they dance, and they want to make audiences feel something, too.

Take the part of Prince Siegfried. He is on stage through four acts. His solos are full of punishing leaps and turns. It might seem to be enough of an achievement to simply pass the endurance test and master the technical intricacies of the performance. (Fernando Bujones says that even at the peak of his career and physical conditioning, he could barely get out of bed the morning after he danced the part of Prince Siegfried. "You feel so broken. I could hardly walk and I thought, What happened to me? Did a truck run over me or something?")·

But a great dancer also has the power to make the audience feel sorry for Prince Siegfried. This isn't easy, because on the surface Siegfried can seem like a very shallow fellow. Why is he so depressed at the beginning of the ballet? He's rich and it's his birthday. Sure he has to choose a wife, but that's hardly unusual for

his time. Why is he sulking like a spoiled brat?

And how can he really believe that the wicked Odile is his beloved Odette? She certainly doesn't act like Odette, and she's dressed in *black*, for heaven's sake.

Male dancers have to give a great deal of thought to making Prince Siegfried's character believable and sympathetic. They know that if *they* don't believe in the character, they certainly won't be able to convince an audience to care about him either.

Igor Zelensky and Zhana Ayxpor in the Kirov's 1992 production of *Swan Lake*

Kevin McKenzie says that to him, the prince is depressed not simply because his carefree bachelor days are over. He's also going to be King. Everywhere he looks, somebody is expecting something from him. The peasants are depending on him to protect them from neighboring enemies. The nobles are eyeing him with suspicion and greed, wondering how to get close to the seat of power. Even his drinking buddies may drop him once his partying days are over. And his cagey mother is watching him closely, perhaps half hoping that he will mess up in his new role.

So, on his twenty-first birthday, it slowly dawns on Siegfried that he has enormous responsibilities and that he is facing them all alone.

Swan Lake: Synopsis

Act I

The kingdom is celebrating Prince Siegfried's twenty-first birthday. The Queen Mother gives her son her own wedding ring as a symbol of his coming of age and then demands that he choose a bride. Reluctant to marry until he is in love, the prince is distressed. His friend Benno leads him off into the forest to hunt swans.

Act II

As Siegfried, now separated from Benno, pursues the swans, a mysterious figure, Von Rothbart, accosts him. He tempts Siegfried by offering him Odette, a pure and divine swan. Odette and Siegfried fall in love.

Act III

At a ball at the palace, Siegfried is presented with many possible princess brides, but he ignores them all. Suddenly Von Rothbart appears with a princess dressed all in black and called Odile, an evil twin of Odette. Siegfried is fooled. As he declares his love for Odile, Odette's cry of betrayal mingles with the triumphant laughter of the scornful Von Rothbarts, who then reveals their true identities. A flood envelops the palace. All but Siegfried are drowned.

Act IV

Siegfried rushes back to the lake, where Odette forgives him. Then, to release herself from the sorcerer's power, she leaps to her death from a high rock into the lake. While Von Rothbart writhes in fury, knowing that true love has triumphed, Siegfried throws himself into the water to be with his love forever.

The Bolshoi Ballet's Maya Plisetskaya

As for the prince being fooled by Odile, this is where the acting and dancing talents of the principal ballerina are put to the test. She must convince the prince, and the audience, that she really *could* be the white swan. Cynthia Gregory says, "I really felt the black swan had to be as much the white swan as possible, otherwise the prince (even a prince blinded by love) looks too stupid. She should have some shred of the white swan, something to make him believe that she is Odette. So I really try to soften her edges every once in a while."

Odette/Odile is such a complicated, difficult role, occasionally it has been danced by two different ballerinas. It's also true that a ballerina usually feels more comfortable with one part than the other. "Very few ballerinas really succeed in showing the two sides of Odette/Odile," says Irina Kolpakova. "Always one is nearer in character to the dancer, and one turns out feeling more natural than the other."

It's sometimes easy to forget, when we watch them perform their superhuman leaps and turns, that the

Rudolf Nureyev and Cynthia Gregory perform in the American Ballet Theater's production of *Swan Lake*

best dancers are also gifted actors. "To be a great actress you don't necessarily have to be able to dance," Marianna Tcherkassky reminds us. "But to be a great ballet dancer you have to be a great actress as well." This is especially true of *Swan Lake*: if the audience can't feel Prince Siegfried's confusion and pain, if they can't pity Odette and hate Von Rothbart, then the ballet is empty and the audience goes away feeling nothing.

Swan Lake is one of the most difficult and most memorable ballets to perform because the members of the corps must stay perfectly in synch

Those @#$%^&* Fouettés!

For a ballerina, the nightmare moment of *Swan Lake* comes when Odile must perform thirty-two consecutive fouettés.

Russians Snub Homegrown Talent

Marius Petipa was hailed as a genius when *Swan Lake, The Sleeping Beauty* and *The Nutcracker* were first performed by the Imperial Ballet of Russia in the late 1800s. But he got more credit than he deserved. The real talent behind at least half of *Swan Lake* and virtually all of *The Nutcracker* was Petipa's assistant, Lev Ivanov. It was Ivanov who developed the idea of a woman trapped in the body of a bird, and it was Ivanov who created the "white" swan scenes with the eerie and sinuous birdlike movements that make *Swan Lake* so unforgettable.

But Petipa was a Frenchman and therefore to be respected. (All things French were aped and admired by the French-speaking Russian court.) Ivanov was merely a Russian.

A fouetté is a spin on one pointe while the other leg snaps around like a whip. Advanced ballet students struggle to master just one fouetté. Yet in the middle of Act III, Odile must do thirty-two of them in a row. Why? Because back in the late 1800s, an Italian ballerina named Pierina Legnani so impressed choreographer Marius Petipa with this feat that he incorporated the spins into the ballet, forcing every ballerina thereafter to do them as well. (Legnani also impressed the audience.

Ballerina Spins Herself Offstage!

Ballerinas still curse Pierina Legnani for showing off to Marius Petipa. "I struggled all my life with those fouettés," says Natalya Makarova, describing her first performance as Odette/Odile with the Kirov Ballet in Leningrad. As she progressed through her fouettés, she gradually began to travel backwards. "After sixteen, I finished in the back wing and totally disappeared. So you can see how much I love them!"

They screamed for more, so she repeated the fouettés — sixty-four in all.) And as dancers struggled to duplicate her accomplishment, they had to look more closely at their own technical abilities. Ballet was becoming more than a display of grace and beauty; dancers were now expected to have athletic prowess as well.

Those fouettés are not only incredibly difficult, ballerinas say, but they are also an irritating disruption to the story. It's as if Odile, in the middle of seducing the Prince, suddenly decided to pull out a bunch of balls and start juggling.

For a ballerina, the pressure of these thirty-two fouettés is enormous. You can practically see the spectators' lips moving as they count each spin. The ballerina can feel the audience mesmerized by that tiny spot where the toe of her supporting foot meets the floor. Will she stay glued to that spot, the crowd wonders, or will she lose control and begin to travel across the stage? Will she make all thirty-two turns, or will she fudge the last couple? Will there be triumph in her eyes at the end, or panic?

Peter Ilyich Tchaikovsky, shortly before his death in 1893. He was only fifty-three years old.

But the fouettés also offer a dancer a unique connection with the audience. If a ballerina has a bit of a hard time, she will hear sympathetic and appreciative applause nonetheless for having made a brave attempt to achieve something that is incredibly difficult. And if she nails every fouetté on a dime, the crowd will rise to its feet and go absolutely wild with cheers.

Tchaikovsky: Miserable Genius

The man who composed the music for three of the world's most famous ballets — *Swan Lake*, *The Nutcracker* and *The Sleeping Beauty* — was a nervous wreck for most of his life. Peter Ilyich Tchaikovsky could have had a decent career as a law clerk. Instead he gave up his job to become a poor music student when he was in his early twenties. He was also a homosexual during a time when homosexuality was considered totally unacceptable, and this made him desperately unhappy. But his confusion and sadness also likely inspired him to produce the most moving ballet music of all time. Before Tchaikovsky, ballet composers

Swan Lake Flops!

When *Swan Lake* was first performed in 1877, it was a disaster. The choreography was a mishmash of dances and even the music was drawn from other ballets. To top it off, the choreography didn't match the music. The ballet was dropped but it wasn't forgotten. Almost twenty years later, Marius Petipa and Lev Ivanov revised *Swan Lake*, and when it was performed again, it was a hit.

What made Marius Petipa go back to a ballet that had been such a failure? When Petipa examined the score closely, he realized that Tchaikovsky's work was brilliant and that the music had to be given another chance.

were considered by many to be nothing but musical hacks. Tchaikovsky made it respectable for serious composers to write for the ballet.

Some critics say his music is overly emotional. But it is this sense of yearning and conflict and the unforgettable melodies that make it perfect for the ballet. Many dancers say it is Tchaikovsky's music that first drew them to ballet. "His music gets inside you," says Veronica Tennant.

Tchaikovsky always considered *Swan Lake* to be a failure, and he blamed himself for its initial lack of success. He committed suicide in 1893, three years before the ballet was relaunched to huge critical acclaim.

Dancing *Swan Lake* with feeling — the National Ballet of Canada

Romeo and Juliet

Perfect Partnerships

Ballet dancers don't approach *Romeo and Juliet* with the same fear they have for the technical nightmares of *The Sleeping Beauty*, or with the weary affection they have for *The Nutcracker*. Instead, dancers love to dance *Romeo and Juliet*.

It's partly Sergei Prokofiev's beautiful music that makes this ballet the all-time favorite of so many dancers. Even more important than the music, however, is the fact that dancers can so easily connect with the everyday, real emotions and situations in *Romeo and Juliet*. The dance steps are natural and reflect the movements of ordinary life, and the story is just as heartbreaking and familiar today as it was when Shakespeare wrote it. Whether it is set in a modern beach town full of punks (the film version with Leonardo DiCaprio and Claire Danes), set in New York City (the musical *West Side Story*), or told strictly through dance, the story of *Romeo and Juliet* still has the ability to move people to tears.

Aleksander Antonijevic in a fight scene of The National Ballet of Canada's production of *Romeo and Juliet*

A costume sketch by Jürgen Rose of Juliet's outfit for The National Ballet of Canada's production of *Romeo and Juliet*

Mikhail Baryshnikov and Kathleen Moore in rehearsal

Anyone can empathize with the story of two young people who are desperately in love but are forbidden to be together. And Juliet is not a doll or a swan or a sleeping princess, but a real teenager who loves clothes, looks forward to a big party and is also capable of deceiving and defying her parents.

What's the secret to portraying a fourteen-year-old girl? How were Natalia Makarova and Margot Fonteyn able to dance this role so convincingly, even when they were in their forties? Ballerinas say it takes much more than to simply dance with the lightness and energy of youth. You have to dance the early scenes of *Romeo and Juliet* with the pure, unwavering optimism of a girl who is certain that things will work out — a girl who, unlike the audience, has no inkling of the tragedy that lies ahead.

Romeo is a plum role for a male dancer, too, largely because it offers a chance to be a complex human being on stage instead of another mushy-eyed prince. Kevin McKenzie, who first danced Romeo later in his career, says the role was a revelation: "For the first time I'm not falling in love with a bird or being danced to death by Wilis or waking up a girl who's been sleeping for a hundred years. It's human … it's real life that happens every day." Romeo is someone that everyone can recognize. He's a dreamer, he gets jealous, he loves a good skirmish and a dirty joke. He flirts with girls and hangs out with his friends, and together they behave like most guys — egging each other on, defending each other, and ultimately even dying and killing for one another.

Kirov Ballet's 1992 production of *Romeo and Juliet*, featuring principal dancers Larissa Lezhnina and Alexander Gulyaev

At the same time, the dancing is intense. "You're on the stage and dominating it for most of the ballet," says McKenzie. "But you're not standing around for a single second. Every minute is high-pitched…. That was a ballet where I was physically sick the next day."

Romeo and Juliet are such juicy roles that some dancers, like actors, will even do homework to help them prepare for their parts. Some watch movie versions of the play. Others read Shakespeare's text to see how his words are reflected in the music and dance steps. One ballerina even carried the play around in her bag, so she could refer to it at a moment's notice while she was preparing for the role.

Other dancers collect modern-day Romeo and Juliet stories as a reminder that this story is still happening all over the world.

Mikhail Baryshnikov and Gelsey Kirkland

(*Far right*) Frank Augustyn and Karen Kain

"Something happens when I get out there, and I feel it right away with my partner, with the audience … something in the air almost, some kind of electricity, and there is complete attention from the audience.… And I know that their attention is really on us and we're really involved in each other and the performance takes off."

— Karen Kain

Rex Harrington and Chan Hon Goh

Rudolf Nureyev and Margot Fonteyn

In Pakistan a young couple are forced to go into hiding after their elopement causes riots among their hostile ethnic groups. In Sarajevo a Serbian boy and his Muslim girlfriend are shot dead as they try to cross battle lines to reach one another.

But more than having a wonderful Juliet and a convincing Romeo, it's the partnership of the two dancers that makes this ballet special. And finding a good dance partnership isn't easy.

Pairing dancers may at first seem quite simple. First you need a correct meshing of body types and height. (Mikhail Baryshnikov has reportedly been dismayed more than once to find a particularly talented ballerina and know that he could never be her partner, simply because she was too tall for him.) Similar dancing styles, technique, attitudes to work and even personalities are also important. Unlike the earlier classical ballets, where the male either dances alone or stands behind the ballerina to support her, the pas de deux in *Romeo and Juliet* are filled with lots of side-by-side dancing, exquisitely timed approaches and complex lifts. Dancers must work *with* each other, not simply alongside each other.

Most dancers will say that a good partnership demands understanding and generosity. Working with a partner requires complete trust, says Darcey Bussell, because a lot of the moves are difficult. "They can be dangerous if performed halfheartedly." And individual dancers must be willing to put their egos aside in order to make their partners look good — not always easy when two superstars are involved. "You don't want to express yourself at the expense of the couple," warns Vladimir Vasiliev.

Great partnerships happen so seldom that when they do appear, the whole ballet world sits up and tries to figure out why they work. With Margot Fonteyn and Rudolf Nureyev many speculated that their partnership was a matter of opposites attracting and complementing each other. She was cool, regal and British. He was rebellious, hot-headed, Russian and twenty years younger. Yet somehow when they danced *Romeo and Juliet*, the audience believed that true love was possible between them.

Sometimes it is physical and musical compatibility that makes the match. Antoinette Sibley and Anthony Dowell had

Romeo and Juliet: Synopsis

Act I, Scene I

The two most powerful families of Verona — the Capulets and the Montagues — are in the midst of a long-standing feud. On the street, playful teasing soon turns into a brawl as members of the opposing families draw swords and begin to fight. The riot is quelled by the Duke of Verona, who decrees banishment if either family disturbs the peace again.

Act I, Scene II

Juliet, the daughter of Lord Capulet, teases her nurse. Her mother brings her the dress she is to wear to her first ball that evening. Excited, she dances about with her dress but stops when she realizes her carefree childhood is coming to an end.

Act I, Scene III

It is the night of the party at the Capulet house. Romeo Montague and his friends, Benvolio and Mercutio, sneak into the party.

Act I, Scene IV

Juliet arrives and is introduced to Count Paris, to whom she is betrothed. While dancing, she and Romeo see one another and fall in love. Tybalt, Juliet's cousin, recognizes Romeo as a Montague and challenges him to a duel.

Act I, Scene V

Later that night, Romeo secretly arrives at Juliet's balcony, and the young lovers swear eternal love to one another.

Act II, Scene I

Juliet's nurse searches for Romeo to give him a note from her mistress. Juliet has agreed to meet Romeo secretly in Friar Laurence's cell where they can be married.

Act II, Scene II

The young lovers are married by Friar Lawrence who hope the union will bring peace between the two feuding families.

Act II, Scene III

Tybalt comes looking for Romeo, but Romeo, knowing that he is now a member of Tybalt's family, refuses to fight. His friend Mercutio agrees to fight on Romeo's behalf, and he is killed in the subsequent duel. In his anger and grief at Mercutio's death, Romeo kills Tybalt.

Act III, Scene I

The Duke of Verona banishes Romeo from Verona for killing Tybalt, but Romeo remains for his wedding night with Juliet. At dawn he leaves. Juliet's parents inform her she is to marry Paris the next day. In desperation, Juliet hurries to seek advice from Friar Laurence.

Act III, Scene II

Friar Laurence gives Juliet a vial containing a sleeping potion that will induce a deathlike coma. He also sends a messenger to tell Romeo what has happened.

Act III, Scene III

Juliet drinks the potion and falls unconscious. In the morning Juliet's bridesmaids find her and presume her dead.

Act III, Scene IV

Juliet is laid to rest in the Capulet vault. Romeo hears of her death but has not yet received Friar Laurence's message. He hurries to her tomb, finds Paris and, in desperation, kills him. Believing Juliet to be dead, he then takes his own life. Juliet wakes up and is horrified to find Romeo lying dead beside her. In her grief, she, too, takes her own life.

body types and styles of movement that matched perfectly and reflected their shared English training. When they moved to the music, they moved as one — "like two wings of the same bird," said one critic.

With the famous Bolshoi duo, Ekaterina Maximova and

Vladimir Vasiliev, it was the spark of shared passion. The dancers were married, and many spectators felt this aspect gave their performances an extra intensity, though it did not always mean their working relationship went smoothly! "We had terrific fights," admits Vasiliev. "People doubted we would stay together." But they never had arguments on stage. "We believed that the stage was a sacred place," says Maximova. (Not all partners manage to keep their arguments off stage. Anna Pavlova, hailed the world over as a vision of grace and loveliness, is known to have slapped her partner in the face, on stage, whenever a lift displeased her. And Rudolf Nureyev, famous for his mercurial temper, once kicked a ballerina when she changed the choreography in the middle of a performance.)

Erik Bruhn once said that what good dance partners create together is far greater than what either dancer could achieve on their own. Yet there is no formula for a great partnership. "When you try to create them, they never work," says Fernando Bujones. "It's chemistry. It's when two people hear music in the same way; when two people look into each other's eyes and do not need to say anything."

Anna Pavlova would have to hold a pose for as long as twenty seconds in the early days of photography, when long exposures were required. Sometimes she was even supported by clotheslines. To make her toes appear more tapered, she would color her shoes with pencil.

Stars Are Born, Not Made

Ballet schools all over the world are filled with hard-working, talented young dancers, and competition for admission to professional schools and for positions in ballet companies is fierce. Yet this system produces relatively few ballet superstars — far fewer than one finds in film, theater, music or sports.

Stardom is elusive and difficult to predict or define for a dancer. Anna Pavlova achieved fame partly because she worked so hard at it. In the beginning of the twentieth century you could not reach an audience of millions simply by performing in film or on television. So she traveled the world for twenty years (from 1911 to 1931), giving more than 4,000 performances. No town was too remote, no auditorium too small.

On the other hand, few people actually saw Vaslav Nijinsky dance. In his case photos, reminiscences and his reputation for madness and scandal helped to make him famous.

Mikhail Baryshnikov made headlines when he left his native Russia and defected to the West. Some dancers are admired for their remarkable technical feats — Darcey Bussell's high extensions, Vladimir Vasiliev's amazing leaps, Maya Plisetskaya's unearthly arm movements.

Anna Pavlova (1882–1931), one of Russia's most prominent and beloved dancers in the early part of the twentieth century

Maya Plisetskaya in a 1977 production of *Isadora*

Too Tall for Juliet

Choreographers often have definite ideas about what their ballets will look like, and they sometimes insist on casting dancers who they think can produce the effect they want. Evelyn Hart, for instance, despite her stellar reputation, was not allowed to dance Juliet in Kenneth MacMillan's production at the American Ballet Theater.

"I begged him to do it," she remembers. "I cried. [But] I was too tall. He said, 'Your mother [Lady Capulet] will be shorter than you.' And I said, 'But my [real-life] mother *is* shorter than I am.' He said, 'I just don't see you in it and it's my production and I'm sorry.' So I never got to do it with American Ballet Theater and it was heartbreaking for me."

In the end, though, a true star simply has a presence that cannot be ignored, and a charisma that cannot be copied or taught. A true star, such as Rudolf Nureyev (who would be accused of hogging the show, even when he was only standing or walking around), is a rarity.

Evelyn Hart

Sergei Prokofiev

By the time he was thirteen, Russian composer, pianist and conductor Sergei Prokofiev had composed four operas, two sonatas, a symphony and several piano pieces. When his country was plunged into political unrest during the Russian Revolution, he went into exile, first in the United States and then in Paris. But he missed his homeland, and in 1933 he returned to Russia, where he was hired to write the score for *Romeo and Juliet* a short time later. Yet many Russians found his music too "Western" and too modern, and for a while his works were not allowed to be performed in his own country.

Sergei Prokofiev (1891–1953), Russian composer, pianist and conductor

From left to right, Margot Fonteyn, Rudolf Nureyev and Carla Fracci accept raves and applause at the curtain call of the La Scala Opera Ballet's 1981 production of *Romeo and Juliet*

Prokofiev was one of the first composers to add humor and mischief to orchestral music (he also composed the famous symphony, *Peter and the Wolf*). Like Adolphe Adam, he used leitmotifs, giving characters their own musical signatures, such as Lord Capulet's thundering entrance music and Juliet's delicate, lilting melody that we hear not only when she is on stage, but also when she is in Romeo's thoughts.

Even after dancing hundreds of performances, Evelyn Hart says there are still moments in *Romeo and Juliet*'s music that move her to tears. "You finish the performance," she says, "and you walk out into the fresh air and all your senses are heightened."

Epilogue

It should have been a great day. Karen Kain and I were driving to Toronto's O'Keefe Centre for our second performance of *Romeo and Juliet*. We were still very young, barely in our twenties, but had been recognized as two talented dancers with promising careers ahead of us. We'd been chosen to dance the lead roles in one of the greatest ballets of the classical repertoire. The night before had been our debut. The audience had been packed with family and friends, and all had assured us that our performance had been wonderful. We'd been relieved and looking forward to the rest of the run. We were on top of the world.

Just before picking up Karen at her house in Cabbagetown, a small neighborhood in Toronto, Canada, I grabbed a copy of that morning's *Globe and Mail*, which I knew would contain a review of our opening performance the previous night. As I drove, Karen sat in the passenger seat and read the piece aloud.

It was a shockingly bad review — cruel, surprisingly personal and utterly devastating for both of us. Karen cried; I drove on in a state of mute despair. Ahead of us, the blank concrete walls of the theater loomed closer and closer.

I parked two blocks away from the stage door. We sat in the car and talked about quitting. Why should we devote our lives to such an incredibly difficult profession when this was the response to our work? Is this what lay ahead for us? Was this the reward for all those punishing years of training and dedication?

When we finally did get out of the car, our minds were made up. We were professionals. We would fulfil our commitment to the

Karen Kain and Frank Augustyn perform in the National Ballet of Canada's production of *Giselle*

company, dance out our contracts — and *then* we would quit.

It was a long walk to that stage door, but eventually we opened it and went inside. Almost instantly we were surrounded by the other members of the company — fellow dancers, coaches, teachers and directors — all of whom wrapped us up in strong arms of support, friendship and faith. Their warmth and caring lifted our spirits and gave us the courage to go back on stage that evening and perform.

So we did. And it was better than we expected. And our performances after that evening continued to get better still.

Perfection is the hidden, lurking word that permeates throughout every aspect of ballet — perfect body, perfect line, perfect timing, perfect performance. But dancers are not just athletes; they are artists and interpreters who must bring to a performance genuine emotion — emotion that is possible only through a life fully lived, pain and passion truly felt.

Ballet has taught me a great deal, and I've been fortunate to be able to transfer many of the lessons I've learned into other aspects of my life. Ballet has taught me how to focus and work with great determination. It has taught me patience, and it has given me the ability to step back from something difficult, gain perspective and take a different and hopefully more successful second approach. It has taught me when to use a mirror to help me improve my technique but also when to turn away from the mirror and let dance reflect what I truly feel inside. And it has taught me that perfection is a dangerous thing to aim for. Over time I have found that as long as you give your very best effort, you can still hold your head high at the end of the day, regardless of what the critics may think.

So don't aim to be perfect. Aim to give everything your absolute best. Listen to the music. And don't forget to turn away from the mirror once in a while and just *feel*.

Oh yes … and always point your feet.

Index